FROM STRUGGLES TO TRIUMPH

THE REMARKABLE JOURNEYS OF 20 EXTRAORDINARY WOMEN

SARIKA DUBEY

Made with ♥ on the Notion Press Platform
www.notionpress.com

"Dedicated to the resilient spirits of all women, who inspire us with their strength, courage, and determination. May this book serve as a beacon of empowerment, reminding you of your limitless potential. Together, we rise."

Contents

Contents

About The Author

Within you reside Durga and Kali. This statement holds true for Sarika Dubey, a resident of Chandauli district in the state of Uttar Pradesh, India. In male-dominated areas of India, stepping forward as a woman is no less than fighting a war. However, Sarika Dubey has proven this notion wrong through her unwavering determination. With her positive social service and excellent thinking, she has continuously worked for the disabled, children and women, not only at the district level but also at the state and national levels. Notably, she was one of the achievers of the title Eurasia World Record in 2018.

Sarika's struggle began in her childhood. Due to societal fears in rural areas, her grandfather stopped her education. However, with the support of her father, she pursued her education by walking miles. Whether it was school or college, she remained the most beloved and outstanding student of her teachers.

In 2015, she graduated from Chhatradhari Singh P.G. College and then moved to Banaras Hindu University for further education. It was during this time that her inclination towards social service grew. She decided to work for the development of women and children in society instead of opting for a government job.

Because of her dedication, outstanding skills and service towards humanity, she was honoured with the National Change Maker Award in 2019. In 2020, she was recognized as a Youth Social Worker, and in 2021 as the "Kashi ki Beti Samman", a Warrior Woman and a National Award as the Best Social Worker by the Constitution Club of Delhi.

In 2023, she was honoured with the Uttar Pradesh Women Empowerment Award by the District Magistrate, Kashi Dharm

Shiromani Alankaran and Dr. APJ Abdul Kalam Sadbhavana Samman and several other awards including a few from Bangalore.

Sarika reveals that in the coming days, through her NGO "Khushi Ki Udaan" (Flight of Happiness), she plans to work diligently and in a planned manner for the upliftment of the poor, orphaned children, women, elderly and disabled individuals.

Preface

In a world that has too often stifled the voices and potential of women, there emerges a collection of remarkable stories that shatter boundaries and defy expectations. "From Struggles to Triumph: The Remarkable Journeys of 20 Extraordinary Women" is a celebration of the indomitable spirit that resides within women from all walks of life. Through this anthology, we embark on a journey of inspiration, resilience and transformation.

Within the pages of this book, you will encounter the awe-inspiring narratives of twenty women who refused to accept the limitations society imposed upon them. These women come from diverse backgrounds, cultures, and experiences, yet they share one common thread: an unwavering determination to rise above adversity and create their own path to success.

From battling societal norms to overcoming personal hardships, these extraordinary women demonstrate what it means to break free from the shackles of limitations. Their stories resonate with the power of dreams, the audacity to challenge conventions, and the courage to persevere in the face of obstacles.

"From Struggles to Triumph: The Remarkable Journeys of 20 Extraordinary Women" is a testament to the remarkable triumphs achieved when women are empowered to unleash their full potential. It is a tribute to the visionaries, the trailblazers, and the unsung heroes who have paved the way for future generations. These stories will leave an indelible mark on your heart, igniting the flame of inspiration and reminding us all of the limitless possibilities that lie within each and every one of us.

As you embark on this transformative journey, may these tales of courage, resilience, and triumph inspire you to break free from the confines of societal expectations, embrace your own unique voice, and embark on your own extraordinary path of triumph and transformation. Let us celebrate these women who have broken boundaries, not only for themselves but for the countless others who follow in their footsteps.

With deep gratitude and admiration for the incredible women who have shared their stories, we invite you to immerse yourself in the empowering world of "From Struggles to Triumph: The Remarkable Journeys of 20 Extraordinary Women."

Sarika Dubey, Chandauli, Uttar Pradesh
sarikaindiag20@gmail.com

ONE

Amrita Sher-Gil: A Pioneer of Modern Indian Art

Amrita Sher-Gil, born on January 30, 1913, in Budapest, Hungary, was an extraordinary artist who left an indelible mark on the world of modern Indian art. Her work, characterized by its boldness, depth, and reflection of Indian culture, continues to be celebrated for its profound artistic expression and unique vision.

Sher-Gil's multicultural upbringing played a significant role in shaping her artistic sensibilities. Her father, Umrao Singh Sher-Gil Majithia, was a Punjabi Sikh aristocrat and scholar, while her mother, Marie Antoinette Gottesmann, was a Hungarian-Jewish opera singer. This diverse heritage provided Sher-Gil with a rich tapestry of influences from both Indian and European traditions.

At a young age, Sher-Gil displayed a natural talent for painting. She received formal art lessons starting at the age of eight and showed remarkable progress in her artistic development. During her early years in Budapest, she often painted the servants in her household, using them as models and capturing their essence on canvas. These early experiences would later inspire her return to India.

In 1921, Sher-Gil's family faced financial difficulties, prompting them to move to Shimla, India. It was here that she further nurtured her artistic abilities, learning the piano, violin, and taking formal painting lessons. Sher-Gil's talent flourished under the guidance of Major Whitmarsh and later Beven Pateman, who provided her with an academic foundation and encouraged her artistic pursuits.

At the age of 16, Sher-Gil embarked on a journey to Europe with her mother to pursue her artistic training. In Paris, she studied at the prestigious Académie de la Grande Chaumière under the tutelage of renowned artists such as Pierre Vaillent and Lucien Simon. Sher-Gil drew inspiration from European masters like Paul Cézanne and Paul Gauguin, while also developing her own distinctive style and voice.

Sher-Gil's time in Paris was transformative. Her paintings exhibited a maturity and conviction rarely seen in someone so young. Her work garnered recognition and acclaim, with her 1932 oil painting titled "Young Girls" serving as a breakthrough piece. It earned her accolades, including a gold medal and the distinction of being the youngest-ever member and the only Asian artist to be elected as an Associate of the Grand Salon in Paris.

Despite her success in Europe, Sher-Gil felt a deep longing to return to India. She believed that her artistic destiny lay within her homeland, where she sought to rediscover and express the essence of Indian life and culture through her paintings. In 1934, she returned to India, marking a significant turning point in her artistic journey.

Sher-Gil's return to India led to a profound shift in her artistic style and subject matter. She immersed herself in the study of Indian art traditions, particularly the Mughal and Pahari schools of painting, as well as the cave paintings at Ajanta. She traveled extensively across India, capturing the diverse landscapes, people, and cultures that inspired her.

Her paintings from this period depict the lives of Indian villagers and women, reflecting a deep empathy for their struggles and aspirations. Sher-Gil's use of vibrant colors and the portrayal of emotions in her subjects revealed her passionate connection to the Indian people. Her works like "Bride's Toilet," "Brahmacharis," and "South Indian Villagers Going to Market" showcased her ability to convey the essence of Indian life with remarkable sensitivity.

In 1939, Sher-Gil married her Hungarian first cousin, Dr. Viktor Egan, and settled in Lahore, undivided India. Her artistic career continued to flourish as she explored new themes and techniques, blending her European training with her deep connection to India. She delved into portraiture, capturing the complexities of individual personalities with remarkable skill. Her self-portraits, in particular, revealed her introspective nature and the struggles she faced as an artist and a woman.

Tragically, Sher-Gil's life was cut short at the age of 28, leaving behind a remarkable body of work that would solidify her status as one of India's most celebrated artists. Her untimely death in 1941 left a void in the art world, but her legacy and impact endured.

Amrita Sher-Gil's contributions to modern Indian art cannot be overstated. She was a pioneer who fearlessly challenged conventions and paved the way for future generations of artists. Her works reflected the complex realities of Indian society, addressing issues of identity, gender, and social inequality. Sher-Gil's art was a bridge between cultures, fusing her European training with her deep-rooted Indian heritage.

Her legacy lives on through her paintings, which continue to inspire and captivate audiences worldwide. Today, her works are celebrated in prestigious galleries and museums, and her influence on Indian art remains profound. Sher-Gil's artistic vision, marked by its raw honesty and emotional depth, transcends time and continues to resonate with viewers.

Amrita Sher-Gil's impact extends beyond her artistic achievements. She played a crucial role in the recognition and appreciation of Indian art globally. By embracing her Indian roots and capturing the essence of Indian life, she challenged the notion that European art was the pinnacle of artistic expression. Sher-Gil's work highlighted the richness and diversity of Indian culture, elevating it to the global stage.

In recognition of her contributions, Sher-Gil was posthumously awarded the Padma Vibhushan, one of India's highest civilian honors, in 1975. Her paintings also fetched record-breaking prices at auctions, further solidifying her stature as an influential and revered artist.

Amrita Sher-Gil's life may have been tragically short, but her artistic legacy continues to inspire artists, art enthusiasts, and cultural historians alike. Her commitment to authenticity, her passion for capturing the essence of Indian life, and her unwavering pursuit of artistic expression make her an icon in the world of modern Indian art. Amrita Sher-Gil will forever be remembered as a trailblazer, a visionary, and a pioneer who reshaped the artistic landscape and left an indelible mark on the history of Indian art.

"Empowered women empower the world; their strength is the cornerstone of progress and equality."

"A woman with a voice is a force to be reckoned with; her words echo the power of change."

TWO

Anandi Gopal Joshi: Pioneering India's First Woman Doctor

Anandi Gopal Joshi holds a significant place in the annals of Indian history as the country's first female physician. Born on March 31, 1865, in Kalyan, Maharashtra, Joshi shattered societal barriers and defied conventions to pave the way for countless women aspiring to pursue a career in medicine. Her remarkable journey and achievements continue to inspire generations.

Joshi's inspiring story begins with her early marriage at the tender age of nine to Gopalrao Joshi, a progressive and supportive husband who believed in educating women. Under his encouragement and guidance, Anandi embarked on a journey that would change the course of her life and contribute to women's empowerment.

Despite facing numerous obstacles, including societal opposition and prevailing gender biases, Joshi's indomitable spirit and determination propelled her forward. She yearned to pursue higher education and become a doctor—a profession unheard of for women in 19th-century India.

With Gopalrao's unwavering support, Joshi's dreams took shape. In 1880, at the age of 14, she set sail for America, where she would embark on her quest for education. Her resolve and ambition led her to enrol at the Women's Medical College of Pennsylvania, making her the first Indian woman to be admitted to a medical school in the United States.

Joshi's journey through medical school was arduous, yet she persevered with unparalleled dedication. Balancing her studies with cultural adjustments and financial constraints, she displayed remarkable resilience in the face of adversity. Joshi's passion for medicine and her strong belief in the power of education sustained her during challenging times.

After four years of rigorous training, Joshi graduated with an MD degree in 1886, accomplishing what many deemed impossible for a woman of her time. Her achievements not only made her a trailblazer for Indian women but also symbolized a triumph over gender-based prejudices prevalent in society.

Eager to serve her homeland, Joshi returned to India, equipped with the knowledge and skills to make a difference. Tragically, her journey was cut short when she succumbed to tuberculosis on February 26, 1887, at the young age of 21. Her untimely demise was a profound loss to the medical fraternity and a reminder of the preciousness of her pioneering efforts.

Anandi Gopal Joshi's legacy, however, transcends her short life. Her unwavering determination, resilience, and groundbreaking achievements continue to inspire generations of women in India and around the world. She laid the foundation for countless women to pursue higher education and break barriers in various fields.

Today, her story serves as a testament to the strength of women and the power of education in transforming lives. Anandi Gopal Joshi's trailblazing journey reminds us that passion, perseverance, and the pursuit of knowledge can conquer even the most formidable obstacles.

As India celebrates its rich history of remarkable women, Anandi Gopal Joshi's name shines brightly, forever etched in the annals of Indian medicine and women's empowerment. Her extraordinary life and pioneering spirit continue to inspire countless individuals to dream big, break barriers, and make a lasting impact on society.

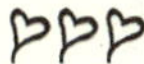

"In the tapestry of life, women are the threads of resilience, weaving dreams into reality."

"The empowerment of women is not just a goal; it's a fundamental right, igniting a brighter tomorrow."

♡♡♡

THREE

ARUNIMA SINHA: FROM THE MOUNTAIN TO THE STARS, DEFYING ALL LIMITS

Arunima Sinha, born on July 20, 1989, in Ambedkar Nagar near Lucknow, Uttar Pradesh, has an inspiring story of resilience and determination. Her father served in the Indian Army, while her mother worked as a supervisor in the health department. Arunima had an elder sister and a younger brother, and her family faced hardships after her father's passing.

Arunima had a passion for sports, particularly football, and she excelled as a national volleyball player. Her dream was to join the paramilitary forces, and she received a call letter from the Central Industrial Security Force (CISF). However, her life took a tragic turn during a journey to Delhi. Robbers attacked her, attempting to snatch her bag and gold chain, and pushed her out of a running train. As a result, she fell onto the track and was unable to move, leading to a train from the opposite direction running over her leg below the knee. The locals immediately rushed her to the hospital, where doctors had to amputate her leg to save her life due to the severity of her injuries.

Following the incident, Arunima received a compensation offer of ?25,000 (US$330) from the Indian Sports Ministry. However, in response to national outrage, the Minister of State for Youth Affairs and Sports, Ajay Maken, announced an additional ?200,000 (US$2,700) as medical relief and recommended a job for her in the CISF. The Indian Railways also offered her employment.

Arunima underwent treatment at the All India Institute of Medical Sciences and was provided with a prosthetic leg free of cost by a Delhi-based company. However, an inquiry by the police raised doubts about her account of the accident, suggesting that she either attempted suicide or had an accident while crossing the railway tracks. Arunima refuted these claims, and the Lucknow bench of the Allahabad High Court ordered the Indian Railways to pay her compensation of ?500,000 (US$6,600).

Despite the challenges she faced, Arunima set her sights on a remarkable goal: climbing Mount Everest. Inspired by cricketer Yuvraj Singh and other stories of resilience, she resolved to achieve something significant in her life. Arunima completed a basic mountaineering course from the Nehru Institute of Mountaineering in Uttarkashi and received encouragement from her mother to pursue her dream of climbing Everest.

She successfully climbed Island Peak (6,150 meters) in 2012 as preparation for her Everest ascent. Joined by Susan Mahout, a USAF instructor, and under the guidance of Hendrick Pal, who had previously climbed Mount Everest, Arunima embarked on her journey to conquer the world's highest peak.

After a grueling 17-hour climb, Arunima reached the summit of Mount Everest at 10:55 AM on May 21, 2013, as part of the Tata Group-sponsored Eco Everest Expedition. This achievement made her the first female amputee to scale Everest. Arunima left a small message of gratitude on a cloth, symbolizing her tribute to Shankara Bhagawan and Swami Vivekananda. Her remarkable feat earned her recognition, and the then-incumbent Chief Minister of Uttar Pradesh, Akhilesh Yadav, honored her with two cheques totaling ?25 lakh at a function in Lucknow. She was also congratulated by the Indian Sports Minister, Jitendra Singh.

Today, Arunima Sinha dedicates herself to social welfare and aims to establish a free sports academy for underprivileged and differently-abled individuals. She selflessly donates the financial aid she receives through awards and seminars to support this cause. The academy, named Shaheed Chandra Shekhar Vikalang Khel Academy, will provide opportunities for sports training to those in need.

Arunima Sinha penned her inspiring story in the book "Born Again on The Mountain," published in 2014. Her accomplishments have been widely recognized, and she was awarded the Padma Shri, the fourth highest civilian award in India, in 2015. Additionally, she received the Tenzing Norgay Highest Mountaineering Award in India, equivalent to the Arjuna Award. Arunima has also set her sights on climbing the highest peaks in all seven continents, and by 2019, she had achieved this goal, becoming the world's first female amputee to climb Mount Vinson in Antarctica.

Arunima Sinha, a true inspiration and a seven-time Indian volleyball player, has overcome immense challenges to prove that with determination, anything is possible. Her indomitable spirit and resilience continue to inspire people around the world.

"Courage knows no gender; women stand tall, breaking barriers, and inspiring generations."

"Empowerment is not a gift; it's a mindset. Women, embrace your strength and rewrite the narrative."

FOUR

Asima Chatterjee: Inspiring Generations

Asima Chatterjee, born on September 23rd, 1917, in Calcutta, India, was a trailblazing Indian organic chemist known for her groundbreaking work in the fields of organic chemistry and phytomedicine. Despite the societal barriers and limited opportunities for women during that time, Chatterjee pursued her passion for education and scientific research.

Coming from a middle-class family, Chatterjee faced the prevailing gender bias that discouraged female education. However, her father, Dr. Indra Narayan Mookerjee, a doctor himself, recognized the importance of education and encouraged Asima and her younger brother to pursue their studies. Her father's love for botany and his interest in medicinal plants sparked Chatterjee's curiosity and fascination with the field of medicine.

In 1936, Chatterjee enrolled in the Scottish Church College at the University of Calcutta, choosing to study chemistry—an uncommon choice for women at the time. She excelled in her studies and graduated with honors distinction. Undeterred by the challenges she faced as a woman in academia, Chatterjee continued her education and obtained her master's degree in organic chemistry from the University of Calcutta in 1938.

Driven by her passion for scientific research, Chatterjee pursued a Doctor of Science (D.Sc.) degree at the University of Calcutta, becoming the first woman to receive a doctorate from an Indian university in 1944. During her doctoral studies, she collaborated with renowned chemists Prafulla Chandra Ray and Satyendra Nath Bose. Chatterjee's research focused on the chemistry of plant products and synthetic organic chemistry.

After completing her doctorate, Chatterjee embarked on post-doctoral research at the University of Wisconsin and the California Institute of Technology (Caltech). She worked under the guidance of Lásló Zechmeister, a prominent chemist, studying biologically active alkaloids.

In 1945, Chatterjee married Professor Baradananda Chatterjee, a physical chemist, and together they had a daughter named Julie. Chatterjee joined the University College of Science at the University of Calcutta as a Reader in pure chemistry. Despite limited government funding and resource constraints, she dedicated herself to researching the nature of biologically active compounds found in medicinal plants. Chatterjee faced numerous challenges, including a lack of necessary chemicals and reagents, and even financed the analysis of her samples outside India using her own funds. Despite these obstacles, she persisted in her scientific pursuits, often struggling to pay her students' salaries.

In 1967, Chatterjee faced a major setback when she tragically lost both her father and husband within a span of four months. Despite this devastating loss and her own health scare, Chatterjee's colleagues provided unwavering support, enabling her to overcome this difficult period and resume her scientific work.

Through her research, Chatterjee made significant contributions to the development of anti-epileptic, anti-convulsive, and chemotherapy drugs. One of her most notable achievements was the development of an anti-epileptic drug called "Ayush-56" from Marsilia minuta, a plant species. This drug remains commercially used to this day. Chatterjee and her team also derived anti-malarial drugs from various plant sources.

Moreover, Chatterjee dedicated over four decades to researching cancer and anti-cancer growth drugs. She conducted extensive studies on a class of compounds known as alkaloids, which demonstrated effectiveness in chemotherapy for cancer patients—an area often considered a dead end for patients at the time.

Chatterjee's groundbreaking work and scientific contributions made her a revered figure in the field of chemistry and phytomedicine. She authored numerous research papers on medicinal plants of the Indian subcontinent and inspired countless women during that era to pursue their dreams and excel as innovators and specialists.

Asima Chatterjee's legacy as a pioneering female scientist and her significant contributions to the field of organic chemistry continues to inspire future generations of researchers, especially women, to push boundaries, challenge norms, and pursue their scientific passions.

"A woman's worth is immeasurable; her abilities, boundless. Empower her, and watch her transform the world."

"Empowered women light the path for others; their brilliance guides us toward a future of equality."

♡♡♡

FIVE

Bhanwari Devi: Journey from Poverty to Empowerment

Bhanwari Devi was born into a Kumhar (potter) family and lived in Bhateri village in the state of Rajasthan, India. The village was predominantly inhabited by the Gurjar community, which held a higher position in the caste hierarchy compared to Bhanwari's family. In the 1990s, child marriages were prevalent in the village, and the caste system played a significant role in societal dynamics.

Bhanwari Devi was married to Mohan Lal Prajapat at a young age, and they had four children together. Bhanwari became a saathin (friend) in 1985 as part of the Women's Development Project (WDP) initiated by the Government of Rajasthan. Her responsibilities as a grassroots worker included addressing issues related to land, water, literacy, healthcare, the Public Distribution System, and fair wages at famine relief works.

In 1992, Bhanwari Devi took up the cause of combating child

marriages, which were still prevalent despite being illegal in India. The Rajasthan state government launched a campaign against child marriage, and Bhanwari actively participated in convincing villagers to refrain from conducting such marriages. However, her efforts faced resistance from the villagers and local leaders, including the village headman.

One particular family, headed by Ram Karan Gurjar, had arranged a child marriage for their nine-month-old daughter. Bhanwari tried persuading them to cancel the wedding, but the marriage took place the following day despite efforts to stop it. The villagers associated the police visits and campaign against child marriage with Bhanwari's actions, leading to social and economic boycotts against her and her family. They faced economic hardships as the villagers refused to sell milk to them or buy their earthen pots. Bhanwari had to leave her job after her employer was assaulted, and her husband was beaten by a member of the Gurjar community.

On September 22, 1992, Bhanwari Devi alleges that she was gang-raped by five men from the Gurjar community while her husband was attacked and rendered unconscious. She filed a police complaint, naming the accused individuals, including those involved in the child marriage she tried to prevent. However, the accused enjoyed support from the local Member of Legislative Assembly (MLA), Dhanraj Meena, who hired a lawyer to defend them.

Bhanwari reported the incident to Rasila Sharma, a block-level worker, who accompanied her to the police station to file a First Information Report (FIR). However, the police showed skepticism and indifference towards her case, which is a common issue faced by rape complainants in South Asia. Bhanwari had to surrender her lehenga (long skirt) as evidence and cover herself with her husband's blood-stained turban to walk to the nearest village.

Indifference continued at the Primary Health Centre (PHC) in Bassi, where the male doctor refused to examine her, and no female doctor was present. She was then referred to Sawai Man Singh (SMS) Hospital in Jaipur, but bureaucratic delays prevented timely medical examination as per legal requirements. Media coverage began after Bhanwari's FIR was published in local and national newspapers.

Bhanwari faced accusations of fabricating the incident, leading to public humiliation in her village. However, women's groups and social organizations in Jaipur began investigating the case, which eventually resulted in a Public Interest Litigation (PIL) filed by the Vishakha collective in the Supreme Court of India. The PIL led to the formulation of the Vishakha Guidelines in 1997, providing definitions of sexual harassment in the workplace and guidelines to address it. The case attracted national and international media attention and became a significant episode in India's women's rights movement.

Bhanwari Devi's struggle against child marriage, her subsequent gang rape, and the subsequent legal and social repercussions shed light on the pervasive issues of gender-based violence, caste discrimination, and the challenges faced by women seeking justice in India. Her case remains an important milestone in the fight for women's rights and serves as a reminder of the obstacles women continue to face in Indian society.

"Strength is not defined by muscles but by the resilience of a woman facing adversity with grace."

"Empowerment is the key that unlocks a woman's potential, turning dreams into achievements."

SIX

CORNELIA SORABJI: PIONEERING JUSTICE

Cornelia Sorabji, a trailblazing figure in the field of law, shattered glass ceilings and defied societal norms to become India's first woman lawyer. Her relentless pursuit of justice, coupled with her unwavering determination, paved the way for generations of women in the legal profession. This chapter explores Cornelia Sorabji's remarkable journey, highlighting her groundbreaking achievements and the enduring impact she has made in the realm of law.

Cornelia Sorabji was born on November 15, 1866, in Nashik, India, into a progressive Parsi family. Despite the prevalent gender bias and limited opportunities for women in her time, Cornelia's father, Reverend Sorabji Karsedji, recognized her exceptional intellect and encouraged her education. This support enabled Cornelia to break free from societal constraints and pursue higher education.

In 1889, Cornelia Sorabji made history by becoming the first woman to graduate from Bombay University, where she excelled in her studies. However, despite her academic prowess, she faced numerous obstacles in pursuing a legal career. At the time, women were barred from practicing law in India, making it a male-dominated profession.

Undeterred by the restrictive norms, Cornelia Sorabji embarked on a relentless quest for justice and women's rights. With the support of influential figures such as Mary Hobhouse, the Countess of Dufferin, and Lord Ripon, Sorabji lobbied for the legal education and empowerment of Indian women.

In 1892, she traveled to England and successfully completed her legal studies at Somerville College, Oxford. Her remarkable achievements paved the way for her to become the first woman to practice law in India.

Cornelia Sorabji dedicated her legal career to championing the rights of women, children, and marginalized communities. As a legal advisor to purdahnashins (women who lived in strict seclusion), Sorabji played a pivotal role in representing their interests and providing them with a voice in legal matters.

Throughout her illustrious career, Sorabji tirelessly fought against social injustice, working towards securing inheritance rights for women and advocating for the improvement of legal protections for widows and children.

Cornelia Sorabji's groundbreaking achievements have left an indelible impact on the legal profession and society as a whole. Her relentless efforts challenged patriarchal norms and opened doors for countless women to pursue careers in law. She paved the way for future generations of women lawyers, who now thrive in the legal profession and continue her legacy of fighting for justice and equality.

Cornelia Sorabji's contributions to the field of law have been widely recognized and honored. In 1904, she was appointed a lady assistant to the Court of Wards, becoming the first woman to hold a government post in British India. Sorabji's groundbreaking work has been celebrated through numerous accolades, including the Kaisar-i-Hind Medal and her induction into the Indian Postal Stamp.

Cornelia Sorabji's extraordinary journey stands as a testament to the power of determination, resilience, and unwavering commitment to justice. By breaking barriers and persistently advocating for the rights of marginalized communities, Sorabji blazed a trail for women in the legal profession and left an enduring legacy of empowerment.

Her pioneering efforts continue to inspire and serve as a reminder that gender should never limit one's aspirations or opportunities. Cornelia Sorabji's story is a beacon of hope, urging us to challenge societal norms, fight for equality, and strive for a more just and inclusive world.

"When women support each other, incredible things happen. Together, they create waves of change."

"A woman's power is her essence; it radiates from within, illuminating the world around her."

♡♡♡

SEVEN

Deepa Malik: A Paralympic Athlete's Inspiring Story

Deepa Malik, a name that resonates with resilience, determination, and the undying spirit to conquer all odds. Born on September 30, 1970, in Sonipat, Haryana, India, Deepa Malik defied societal expectations and shattered barriers to become one of the most celebrated Paralympic athletes in the world. This chapter delves into her extraordinary journey, highlighting her achievements, challenges, and the indomitable spirit that propelled her to success.

Deepa Malik's life took an unexpected turn when, at the age of six, she was diagnosed with a spinal tumor. The diagnosis brought a wave of uncertainty and fear to her family, as the medical condition led to her paralysis from the waist down. However, rather than succumbing to despair, Deepa's family rallied around her, providing unwavering support and encouragement.

Despite facing immense physical challenges, Deepa's indomitable spirit began to shine through. She refused to let her disability define her, and with the support of her family, she resolved to carve her own path. Deepa Malik firmly believed that disability should never hinder one's dreams, and she embarked on a remarkable journey of self-discovery.

Deepa's foray into the world of sports began when she discovered her love for swimming. The pool became her sanctuary, a place where she found solace and a sense of freedom. Her passion for swimming grew, and she started participating in various state-level swimming competitions. Deepa's sheer determination propelled her forward, leading her to win numerous accolades at the national level.

While swimming remained an integral part of her life, Deepa Malik's thirst for new challenges led her to explore other sports as well. She ventured into javelin throw and shot put, displaying exceptional talent and a remarkable work ethic. Her dedication and perseverance paid off when she won a bronze medal in the javelin throw event at the 2010 Para Asian Games, marking her debut on the international stage.

Deepa Malik's breakthrough came at the 2016 Paralympic Games held in Rio de Janeiro, Brazil. This milestone event showcased her unyielding determination and solidified her status as a sporting icon. Deepa competed in the shot put event and secured a silver medal, becoming the first Indian woman to win a Paralympic medal.

Her remarkable achievement not only brought glory to India but also shattered stereotypes surrounding disability. Deepa's triumph inspired countless individuals, proving that disability should never limit one's aspirations or potential. She became a beacon of hope and a symbol of empowerment for people facing physical challenges worldwide.

Deepa Malik's journey extends far beyond her sporting achievements. She is a relentless advocate for inclusivity and accessibility, working tirelessly to create opportunities for individuals with disabilities. Deepa uses her platform to promote a more inclusive society, emphasizing the importance of equal rights and opportunities for all.

As a motivational speaker, Deepa Malik captivates audiences with her inspiring stories of resilience and overcoming obstacles. She encourages individuals to embrace their uniqueness and push beyond their perceived limitations. Deepa's positive outlook on life and unwavering determination have made her a role model for aspiring athletes, individuals with disabilities, and the wider community alike.

In recognition of her outstanding contributions, Deepa Malik has received numerous accolades and awards. She was honored with the prestigious Rajiv Gandhi Khel Ratna award, India's highest sporting honor, in 2019. Deepa's remarkable journey continues to inspire and uplift, leaving an indelible mark on the world of sports and beyond.

Deepa Malik's life is a testament to the power of the human spirit and the triumph of resilience over adversity. From being diagnosed with a spinal tumor at a young age to becoming the first Indian woman to win a Paralympic medal, Deepa's journey is a source of inspiration for people from all walks of life.

Her unwavering determination, combined with her passion for sports, propelled Deepa Malik to achieve greatness. But her impact extends far beyond the realm of sports. Deepa's advocacy work, motivational speaking, and dedication to inclusivity have helped break down barriers and challenge societal norms.

Deepa Malik's story reminds us that our limitations are only as strong as the power we give them. She serves as a guiding light, encouraging us to embrace challenges, chase our dreams relentlessly, and redefine our own potential. Deepa Malik's legacy will continue to inspire generations to come, leaving an indelible mark on the annals of sporting history and beyond.

"Empowered women redefine the standards; they challenge the norm and pave the way for progress."

"The empowerment of women is society's greatest asset; it fosters growth, compassion, and harmony."

♡♡♡

EIGHT

Harnaaz Sandhu: Crowning Glory

In today's fast-paced world, the youth are in search of role models, individuals whose stories inspire and motivate them to overcome obstacles and chase their dreams relentlessly. One such inspiring figure is Harnaaz Sandhu, a name synonymous with grace, determination, and unwavering spirit.

Harnaaz Sandhu is an Indian model, actress, and beauty pageant titleholder who was crowned Miss Universe 2021. She was born on March 3, 2000. Sandhu, who hails from the village of Kohali in Gurdaspur district, Punjab, was previously crowned Miss Diva Universe 2021. She is the third Indian entrant to win the Miss Universe title. Sandhu comes from a Jat Sikh family, and her parents are Pritampal Singh Sandhu, a realtor, and Rabinder Kaur Sandhu, a gynecologist. She has an elder brother named Harnoor.

Sandhu's family moved to England in 2006 and returned to India two years later, settling in Chandigarh, where she grew up. She attended Shivalik Public School and the Post Graduate Government College for Girls in Chandigarh. Before winning Miss Universe, Sandhu was pursuing a master's degree in public administration. She is fluent in Punjabi, Hindi, and English. Sandhu started participating in pageantry as a teenager and won titles such as Miss Chandigarh 2017 and Miss Max Emerging Star India 2018.

After winning the title of Femina Miss India Punjab 2019, Sandhu competed in Femina Miss India and placed in the Top 12. She then participated in the Miss Diva 2021 competition and emerged as one of the Top 20 finalists. During the preliminary competition, she won the Miss Beautiful Skin award and became a finalist for other categories. In the opening statement round of the grand finale, Sandhu spoke about her journey from facing mental health issues, bullying, and body shaming to becoming a confident and compassionate woman who aspires to inspire the youth.

In the final question and answer round, Sandhu spoke about global warming and climate change, emphasizing the need for collective action to preserve the environment. At the end of the event, she was crowned Miss Universe 2021 by the outgoing titleholder. As Miss Universe, Sandhu will reside in New York City and represent India at various events and appearances worldwide. She has already traveled to Israel, the United States, and India in her capacity as Miss Universe.

Harnaaz Sandhu's upbringing was marked by challenges, but it was precisely these challenges that molded her into the strong and resilient individual she is today.

Education became Harnaaz's weapon of choice, empowering her to break barriers and shatter stereotypes. Her dedication to learning serves as a beacon of hope for the new generation, emphasizing the importance of education in today's world.

Harnaaz Sandhu's journey in the world of pageantry was not just about winning crowns but also about making a difference. Her advocacy for various causes showcases the power of using influence for the greater good, teaching the youth the significance of social responsibility.

Confidence radiates from Harnaaz Sandhu, reminding the youth that self-belief is the cornerstone of achieving one's goals. Her leadership qualities inspire the new generation to step into leadership roles fearlessly, believing in their capabilities.

Harnaaz Sandhu challenged societal norms and redefined beauty standards. Her journey serves as a powerful lesson for the new generation, encouraging them to embrace their uniqueness and celebrate diversity.

Life is not without its challenges, and Harnaaz Sandhu's story exemplifies the importance of perseverance. Through her experiences, she teaches the youth the value of grit, reminding them that setbacks are just stepping stones to success.

In a world often dominated by individualism, Harnaaz Sandhu's compassionate nature stands out. Her ability to empathize and connect with people from all walks of life teaches the new generation the significance of fostering genuine human connections.

Despite her achievements, Harnaaz Sandhu remains grounded and humble. Her humility teaches the youth that ambition can coexist with modesty, encouraging them to pursue their dreams while staying true to their roots.

Harnaaz Sandhu's story ignites the spark of ambition in the hearts of the new generation. Her journey encourages them to dream big, reminding them that with dedication and hard work, any aspiration is within reach.

Criticism is inevitable, especially for those in the public eye. Harnaaz Sandhu's ability to handle criticism with grace and poise teaches the youth the importance of resilience, showing them that their worth is not determined by others' opinions.

In the pursuit of success, mental health often takes a back seat. Harnaaz Sandhu's emphasis on mindfulness and well-being serves as a crucial lesson for the new generation, highlighting the importance of mental health in achieving overall success.

Behind every successful individual is a supportive family. Harnaaz Sandhu's close-knit family serves as a reminder to the youth of the importance of family support, emphasizing the role of a strong support system in one's journey.

Harnaaz Sandhu's global recognition showcases the impact one person can have on a global scale. Her story inspires the new generation to think beyond borders, encouraging them to make a difference not only locally but also internationally.

In the age of social media, Harnaaz Sandhu effectively uses her influence for positive change. Her digital presence teaches the youth about responsible social media usage, inspiring them to leverage online platforms to spread positivity and awareness.

In conclusion, Harnaaz Sandhu's journey is a testament to the power of resilience, determination, and kindness. Her inspirational story serves as a guiding light for the new generation, reminding them that no dream is too big and no obstacle insurmountable. As the youth embark on their own journeys, they can find solace and motivation in the remarkable tale of Harnaaz Sandhu.

"A strong woman lifts others up; her kindness and determination create ripples of empowerment."

"Empowerment begins within; women, embrace your worth, and watch the world transform around you."

♡♡♡

NINE

INDIRA JAISING: CHAMPIONING JUSTICE, DEFYING ODDS

Indira Jaising, born on 3 June 1940 in Mumbai, hails from a Sindhi Hindu family. She received her school education in Mumbai and later pursued a Bachelor of Arts degree from Bangalore University. In 1962, she completed her post-graduate law degree (LLM) from the University of Bombay.

In 1981, Jaising, along with her husband Anand Grover, established the Lawyers Collective, a non-governmental organization (NGO) dedicated to feminist and left-wing causes. Her commitment to feminism and her strong personality caught the attention of Sonia Gandhi. In 2009, Jaising became the first woman to be appointed Additional Solicitor General of India, earning recognition for her legal expertise and dedication to human rights and women's rights.

Throughout her legal career, Jaising has been focused on the protection of human rights and the empowerment of women. She has argued numerous cases related to women's discrimination, including landmark cases such as Mary Roy's case, which resulted in equal inheritance rights for Syrian Christian women in Kerala. She also represented Rupan Deol Bajaj, an IAS officer who successfully prosecuted KPS Gill for sexual harassment, marking one of the first successful cases of its kind. Jaising played a pivotal role in the case of Githa Hariharan, where the Supreme Court affirmed that under Hindu law, the mother is considered the "natural guardian" of her minor children, allowing the children to bear their mother's name. Additionally, she challenged discriminatory provisions of the Indian Divorce Act in the High Court of Kerala, securing the right for Christian women to obtain a divorce on grounds of cruelty or desertion.

Jaising has been involved in several significant cases. In 2015, she represented Priya Pillai in the Greenpeace India case. In 2016, she challenged the procedure for designating senior advocates in the Supreme Court. Jaising has also advocated for the victims of the Bhopal tragedy in their quest for compensation from the American multinational Union Carbide Corporation. She has taken up cases for homeless pavement dwellers in Mumbai facing eviction and has been an active environmentalist, arguing major environmental cases in the Supreme Court.

Jaising's dedication to justice extends beyond national boundaries. She has served on various People's Commissions on Violence in Punjab, investigating extra-judicial killings, disappearances, and mass cremations that occurred from 1979 to 1990. The United Nations appointed Jaising and two other experts to a fact-finding mission investigating alleged human rights violations against Rohingya Muslims in Myanmar's Rakhine state.

Jaising's commitment to social justice led her to establish the Lawyers Collective, an organization that provides legal aid and support to marginalized sections of Indian society. She also founded a monthly magazine called The Lawyers in 1986, focusing on social justice and women's issues within the Indian legal context.

Jaising has actively fought against child labor, advocated for the economic rights of women, and taken up cases related to estranged wives and domestic violence. Her efforts have garnered national and international recognition, with her representation of India at various women-focused conferences.

Jaising's contributions have earned her accolades and honors. She was awarded the Padma Shree by the President of India in 2005 for her significant contributions to public affairs. She received the Rotary Manav Seva Award in recognition of her fight against corruption and her advocacy for the marginalized sections of society.

It is important to note that the Lawyers Collective, the NGO founded by Jaising, faced challenges regarding its foreign funding and violation of the Foreign Contribution Regulation Act (FCRA). The Indian government canceled the NGO's license permanently, citing the utilization of foreign funds for purposes not mentioned in its objectives. However, the Bombay High Court ordered the domestic accounts of the NGO to be unfrozen, providing some relief. The case is still ongoing in the Supreme Court of India, and further legal proceedings will determine the outcome.

Indira Jaising is an influential legal activist known for her tireless efforts in promoting human rights causes, particularly women's rights. Her dedication, legal acumen, and relentless pursuit of justice have positioned her as a prominent figure in the Indian legal landscape.

"The empowerment of women is not just a movement; it's a revolution, reshaping the world for the better."

"A woman's dreams know no bounds; empower her, and she will reach for the stars, inspiring others to follow."

♡♡♡

TEN

Irom Chanu Sharmila: Iron Lady of Manipur

Irom Chanu Sharmila, also known as the "Iron Lady of Manipur" or "Mengoubi," is an Indian civil rights activist, political activist, and poet from the state of Manipur. Born on March 14, 1972, in Manipur, a state in northeast India that has experienced a prolonged insurgency, Sharmila grew up in a region plagued by political violence, with thousands of deaths reported between 2005 and 2015.

Sharmila became involved in local peace movements advocating for human rights in Manipur. Her activism gained momentum after the "Malom Massacre" on November 2, 2000, when ten civilians were shot and killed by the Assam Rifles, an Indian paramilitary force operating in the state. In response, Sharmila started a hunger strike demanding the repeal of the Armed Forces (Special Powers) Act (AFSPA), which grants security forces sweeping powers in the region. She vowed not to eat, drink, comb her hair, or look in a mirror until the AFSPA was repealed.

Shortly after beginning her fast, Sharmila was arrested by the police and charged with an "attempt to commit suicide," as it was deemed unlawful under the Indian Penal Code at that time. She was placed under judicial custody, and her health rapidly deteriorated. To keep her alive while under arrest, nasogastric intubation was forced upon her.

Over the years, Sharmila has been released and re-arrested multiple times, but her hunger strike persisted. She became an icon of public resistance and garnered international support. In 2016, after fasting for 16 years, she ended her hunger strike on August 9 and announced her intention to enter politics. Sharmila aimed to fight for the removal of the AFSPA and joined the political arena, vowing to continue her struggle.

Sharmila's life and activism have been the subject of books, including "Burning Bright: Irom Sharmila and the Struggle for Peace in Manipur" by Deepti Priya Mehrotra, and adaptations for theater performances. She married her British partner, Desmond Anthony Bellarnine Coutinho, in 2017 and gave birth to twin daughters named Nix Shakhi and Autumn Tara in 2019.

Despite facing challenges, legal battles, and being declared a prisoner of conscience by Amnesty International, Irom Sharmila remains an influential figure in the fight for human rights and the repeal of the AFSPA in Manipur. Her dedication and resilience have made her a symbol of courage and determination in India and beyond.

"Empowered women stand as beacons of hope, illuminating the path toward a more inclusive and just society."

"Every woman has a story, a voice, and a purpose. Empowerment amplifies her voice, making her story resonate across the universe."

♡♡♡

ELEVEN

Kadambini Ganguly: Pioneering Paths in Medicine

Kadambini Ganguly, a name etched in the annals of Indian history, emerged as a trailblazer in the field of medicine. She shattered societal norms and became one of India's first female graduates and doctors, paving the way for women's education and empowerment. This chapter delves into the remarkable life and achievements of Kadambini Ganguly, highlighting her groundbreaking journey in the medical field and her enduring impact on society.

Kadambini Ganguly was born on July 18, 1861, in Bhagalpur, Bihar, during a time when women's education was severely restricted. Despite the prevailing social barriers, Kadambini's progressive-minded family recognized the importance of education and supported her intellectual pursuits. She pursued her education with determination, setting the stage for her pioneering journey.

In 1883, Kadambini Ganguly created history by becoming one of the first two female graduates in India. She completed her Bachelor of Arts degree from Bethune College, Kolkata, setting a precedent for women's higher education in the country. Kadambini's achievement challenged the prevailing notion that education was solely meant for men.

Fuelled by her passion for knowledge and a desire to serve humanity, Kadambini Ganguly set her sights on the medical profession. However, her aspirations faced numerous hurdles, as medical education and practice were largely inaccessible to women at the time.

Undeterred by the challenges, Kadambini Ganguly fought for her right to pursue medicine. In 1886, she became one of the first female students to be admitted to the Calcutta Medical College, breaking new ground for women in the field of medicine. Her admission marked a significant milestone, paving the way for future generations of women doctors in India.

Kadambini Ganguly's pioneering journey in medicine inspired countless women to follow in her footsteps. She challenged societal norms, paving the way for women's education and empowerment in India. Her accomplishments motivated other women to pursue careers in medicine, fostering a sense of hope and breaking down barriers that restricted their potential.

Kadambini Ganguly's journey extended beyond her groundbreaking achievements in education and medicine. She dedicated her life to serving society, particularly marginalized communities. She worked tirelessly to improve healthcare facilities for women and children, addressing the pressing healthcare needs of her time.

Kadambini Ganguly's remarkable achievements garnered widespread recognition and respect. Her unwavering commitment to education, women's empowerment, and healthcare reform made her an iconic figure in Indian history. Her legacy continues to inspire generations of women to dream big, strive for excellence, and contribute to the betterment of society.

Kadambini Ganguly's indomitable spirit and unwavering determination challenged societal norms and carved a path of progress for women in India. Her historic accomplishments in education and medicine opened doors that had long been closed, enabling countless women to pursue their dreams in fields that were once deemed off-limits.

Her legacy serves as a reminder that with perseverance, resilience, and a relentless pursuit of knowledge, barriers can be overcome, and transformative change can be achieved. Kadambini Ganguly's inspiring journey continues to empower women, emphasizing the importance of education, gender equality, and service to society.

Her story encourages us to challenge conventional boundaries, embrace opportunities, and strive for equality in all aspects of life. Kadambini Ganguly's legacy will forever shine as a beacon of hope, igniting the flames of courage and determination in those who dare to dream and make a difference.

"Empowerment is the gift women give themselves, a spark that ignites the flames of change."

"A woman empowered knows no limits; she is a force of nature, fierce and unstoppable."

♡♡♡

TWELVE

KIRAN MAZUMDAR-SHAW: THE ENTREPRENEURIAL ODYSSEY

Kiran Mazumdar-Shaw, born on March 23, 1953, in Bangalore, Karnataka, India, is an Indian billionaire entrepreneur and the executive chairperson and founder of Biocon Limited and Biocon Biologics Limited. She is also the former chairperson of the Indian Institute of Management, Bangalore.

Mazumdar-Shaw was educated at Bishop Cotton Girl's High School and Mount Carmel College in Bangalore, where she studied biology and zoology. She graduated from Bangalore University in 1973 with a bachelor's degree in zoology. Initially, she aspired to attend medical school but was unable to secure a scholarship.

Her father, Rasendra Mazumdar, who worked as the head

brewmaster at United Breweries, suggested that she study fermentation science and become a brewmaster, which was an unconventional field for women. Mazumdar-Shaw went to Ballarat College, Melbourne University in Australia to study malting and brewing. In 1974, she became the only woman enrolled in the brewing course and excelled, earning a master brewer degree in 1975.

After working as a trainee brewer and maltster in Australia, she returned to India and started Biocon India in 1978. With a seed capital of Rs. 10,000, she established the company in the garage of her rented house in Bangalore. Initially facing credibility challenges due to her youth, gender, and untested business model, Mazumdar-Shaw struggled to secure funding and recruit employees. However, she persevered and became the first Indian company to manufacture enzymes and export them to the United States and Europe.

Under Mazumdar-Shaw's leadership, Biocon evolved from an industrial enzymes manufacturing company to a fully integrated bio-pharmaceutical company with a focus on diabetes, oncology, and auto-immune diseases. She also established subsidiaries, including Syngene, which provides research and development support services, and Clinigene, which focuses on clinical research trials and the development of medicines. Biocon's IPO in 2004 was oversubscribed 33 times, making it the second Indian company to cross the $1 billion mark on the first day of listing.

Mazumdar-Shaw has actively engaged in acquisitions, partnerships, and licensing deals in the pharmaceutical and bio-pharmaceutical sectors. She has also established the Biocon Foundation, which focuses on health, education, and infrastructure in rural areas of Karnataka.

She is known for her philanthropic efforts and prefers the term "compassionate capitalist" over "philanthropy." In 2015, she joined The Giving Pledge, committing to donate at least half of her wealth to philanthropic causes.

Mazumdar-Shaw has received numerous national and international awards, including the Padma Shri and Padma Bhushan from the government of India. She has been recognized as the "Global Indian Woman of the Year" and "Businesswoman of the Year," among other accolades. In 2019, Forbes listed her as the 68th most powerful woman in the world, and she was named the EY World Entrepreneur Of The Year in 2020.

She is married to John Shaw, and she continues to make significant contributions to the field of biotechnology and business in India.

"In the tapestry of empowerment, every woman is a vibrant thread, weaving a story of strength and resilience."

"Empowering women isn't just a mission; it's a movement that transforms societies and hearts."

♡♡♡

THIRTEEN

Mrinalini Sarabhai: Dancing Through Life

In the annals of Indian history, certain individuals shine brightly as beacons of inspiration, guiding generations with their exceptional contributions. One such luminary is Mrinalini Sarabhai, a woman whose life was an extraordinary tapestry of dance, education, and social reform.

Mrinalini Sarabhai was born on May 11, 1918, in present-day Kerala, India. Her father, Subbarama Swaminathan, was a distinguished lawyer, and her mother, A.V. Ammukutty, was a social worker and independence activist. She received her early education at a boarding school in Switzerland, where she was exposed to the Dalcroze school of dance movements. Later, she studied at Shantiniketan under the guidance of Rabindranath Tagore, which played a crucial role in shaping her artistic journey.

After a brief period in the United States, where she attended the

American Academy of Dramatic Arts, Mrinalini returned to India and began her training in Bharatanatyam, a south Indian classical dance form, under Meenakshisundaram Pillai. She also studied the classical dance-drama of Kathakali under the renowned Guru Thakazhi Kunchu Kurup. In 1942, she married Vikram Sarabhai, an Indian physicist known as the Father of the Indian Space Program. They had two children, Kartikeya and Mallika, both of whom later gained fame in dance and theater.

In 1948, Mrinalini founded the Darpana Academy of Performing Arts in Ahmedabad. The academy became an esteemed institution for training in dance, drama, music, and puppetry. A year later, she performed at the Théâtre National de Chaillot in Paris, where she received critical acclaim.

Although Mrinalini and Vikram Sarabhai had a troubled marriage, she continued to pursue her passion for dance and choreography. Besides choreographing over 300 dance dramas, she also wrote novels, poetry, plays, and stories for children. She served as the chairperson of the Gujarat State Handicrafts and Handloom Development Corporation Ltd. and was involved with organizations promoting Gandhian ideals and development. Her autobiography, titled "Mrinalini Sarabhai: The Voice of the Heart," reflects her remarkable journey.

At a time when traditional dance forms faced challenges, Mrinalini Sarabhai played a pivotal role in reviving Bharatanatyam. Her innovative choreography and dedication to preserving the art form breathed new life into classical dance, earning her acclaim and admiration.

Mrinalini Sarabhai believed in the transformative power of dance as a medium for social change. She fearlessly choreographed performances addressing societal issues, advocating for gender equality, environmental conservation, and human rights. Her performances became a catalyst for meaningful dialogue, inspiring audiences to reflect on pressing issues.

Innovation was the cornerstone of Mrinalini Sarabhai's artistic pursuits. She fearlessly experimented with dance, seamlessly blending traditional elements with contemporary expressions. Her avant-garde approach pushed the boundaries of classical dance, captivating audiences and fellow artists alike.

Beyond the stage, Mrinalini Sarabhai was a vocal activist, advocating for the rights of the marginalized and downtrodden. Her relentless efforts in social activism resonated far and wide, establishing her as a compassionate advocate for those often unheard.

Mrinalini Sarabhai's artistry transcended geographical boundaries, earning her international acclaim. She toured extensively, showcasing the rich cultural heritage of India to global audiences. Through her performances, she bridged cultures, fostering mutual understanding and appreciation.

Mrinalini Sarabhai's philanthropic endeavors extended beyond dance. She actively supported educational initiatives, believing in the transformative power of education. Her charitable contributions laid the foundation for schools and programs that continue to empower underprivileged children today.

Recognized for her contributions to art, Mrinalini received several prestigious awards, including the Padma Bhushan in 1992 and the Padma Shri in 1965. Throughout her career, she trained over 18,000 students in Bharatanatyam and Kathakali. She passed away on January 21, 2016, at the age of 97.

"A woman's power is her authenticity; when she embraces it, she inspires others to do the same."

"Empowered women don't just break glass ceilings; they shatter stereotypes and create new possibilities."

♡♡♡

FOURTEEN

MUTHULAKSHMI REDDY: REMARKABLE JOURNEY IN SOCIAL REFORM

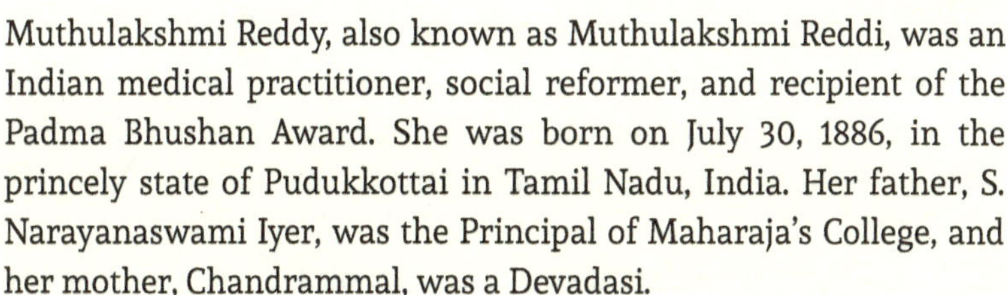

Muthulakshmi Reddy, also known as Muthulakshmi Reddi, was an Indian medical practitioner, social reformer, and recipient of the Padma Bhushan Award. She was born on July 30, 1886, in the princely state of Pudukkottai in Tamil Nadu, India. Her father, S. Narayanaswami Iyer, was the Principal of Maharaja's College, and her mother, Chandrammal, was a Devadasi.

Despite societal constraints faced by girls during that time in India, Muthulakshmi was sent to school by her father, who broke the tradition and supported her education. She excelled in her studies, and in 1907, she joined the Madras Medical College, where she achieved a remarkable academic record. Graduating in 1912, she became one of the first female doctors in India, earning several gold medals and prizes during her time in college.

Muthulakshmi came under the influence of prominent figures like Annie Besant and Mahatma Gandhi, which further shaped her beliefs and activism. In 1914, she married Sundara Reddy, and they had a marriage based on the promise of mutual respect and equality. Following her marriage, she adopted the surname "Reddy." Muthulakshmi had a significant impact on women's rights and social reform during her lifetime.

She had many notable achievements and firsts to her name. She was the first female student to be admitted to a men's college, the first woman House Surgeon at the Government Maternity and Ophthalmic Hospital, the first woman legislator in British India, the first Chairperson of the State Social Welfare Advisory Board, the first woman Deputy President of the Legislative Council, and the first Alderwoman of the Madras Corporation Avvai Home.

Muthulakshmi Reddy's contributions extended beyond her medical profession. She worked tirelessly for women's emancipation and advocated for the rights of women and children. She played a role in the Tamil music movement, worked for the development of the Tamil language, and campaigned for better salaries for Tamil teachers and writers. She also served as the editor of the monthly magazine 'Sthree Dharumam,' which was dedicated to women's issues and published by the Indian Women Association.

In 1926, Muthulakshmi Reddy was appointed to the Madras Legislative Council, marking the beginning of her lifelong efforts to address social abuses, promote equality, and uplift women. Her name was included in the first national flag hoisted on the Red Fort in 1947, symbolizing her significant contributions to the nation.

Muthulakshmi Reddy passed away on July 22, 1968, leaving behind a lasting legacy as a women's activist, social reformer, and advocate for equality and justice.

ღღღ

"The true essence of a society's progress lies in how it empowers its women; they are the backbone of a thriving nation."

"Empowerment is not about giving power; it's about reminding women that they had it all along."

♡♡♡

FIFTEEN

RANI RAMPAL: RISING FROM ADVERSITY

Rani Rampal, the name that echoes through the annals of Indian hockey, represents resilience, passion, and unwavering determination. Born on December 4, 1994, in Shahbad, Haryana, Rani Rampal emerged from humble beginnings to become one of the most prominent figures in Indian sports. This chapter delves into her inspiring journey, highlighting her rise to prominence, the challenges she faced, and the indomitable spirit that led her to captain the Indian women's hockey team.

Rani Rampal's journey began in a small village in Shahbad, where she was introduced to the world of hockey at a tender age. Coming from a financially disadvantaged background, Rani's family struggled to make ends meet. However, her love for the sport and her innate talent fueled her determination to succeed.

Recognizing Rani's potential, her family rallied behind her dreams, offering unwavering support and encouragement. They sacrificed their own comforts to ensure that she had the necessary resources to pursue her passion. Rani's parents, despite the financial challenges they faced, were determined to give their daughter the opportunity to shine on the hockey field.

Rani Rampal's talent on the hockey field quickly became apparent. Her dedication and hard work caught the attention of coaches and selectors, and she earned a place in the junior national team at the age of 14. Rani's performances were nothing short of extraordinary, as she consistently showcased her skills and led her team to numerous victories.

Her exceptional skills did not go unnoticed, and in 2010, at the age of 15, Rani became the youngest player to represent the Indian women's hockey team in an international tournament. Her debut marked the beginning of a remarkable journey that would see her rise through the ranks and become a stalwart of Indian hockey.

Rani Rampal's leadership qualities were evident from the outset. Her unwavering commitment, resilience, and ability to lead by example earned her the captain's armband for the Indian women's hockey team in 2018. As captain, Rani's influence on the team was profound. She instilled a sense of belief and unity among her teammates, fostering a strong team spirit and a winning mentality.

Under Rani's captaincy, the Indian women's hockey team achieved numerous milestones. They secured their place in the 2020 Tokyo Olympics after a gap of 36 years, showcasing their resurgence on the global stage. Rani's leadership propelled the team to success in various international tournaments, including the Asian Games, where they won a silver medal in 2018.

Rani Rampal's journey has not only been about hockey; it has also been about breaking stereotypes and inspiring millions. Coming from a background where societal norms and gender biases often limit opportunities, Rani defied the odds and shattered barriers.

She has become a role model for young girls across India, proving that hard work, determination, and perseverance can overcome any obstacle. Rani's success on the hockey field has challenged the perception of women's sports and has paved the way for a new generation of aspiring athletes to dream big and reach for the stars.

Off the field, Rani Rampal has been actively involved in various social initiatives, using her platform to advocate for gender equality and women's empowerment. She believes in the power of education and works towards providing opportunities for underprivileged children to pursue their dreams.

Rani Rampal's journey from a small village to the captaincy of the Indian women's hockey team is a testament to the power of passion and perseverance. Her rise to prominence, despite financial challenges and societal expectations, exemplifies the indomitable spirit of the human will.

As a beacon of inspiration, Rani Rampal has become a symbol of hope for aspiring athletes and young girls across the nation. Her achievements on the hockey field and her relentless pursuit of excellence have broken barriers and paved the way for a more inclusive and empowered society.

Rani Rampal's story reminds us that greatness knows no boundaries and that with unwavering determination, one can overcome any adversity. She continues to inspire, leaving an indelible mark on the world of sports and serving as a guiding light for generations to come.

"A woman's strength lies in her ability to stand tall even in the face of adversity; that resilience is her superpower."

"Empowerment is not an option; it's a fundamental right, a compass guiding women to their fullest potential."

♡♡♡

SIXTEEN

Rashmi Bansal: Empowering Dreams

Rashmi Bansal, a name synonymous with inspiration and empowerment, is an accomplished author and entrepreneur who has touched the lives of countless individuals through her impactful books. Born in Mumbai, India, Rashmi Bansal has dedicated her career to showcasing the real-life stories of ordinary people who have achieved extraordinary success against all odds. This chapter explores her literary journey, focusing on her motivational books and her dedication to empowering women to pursue their dreams.

Rashmi Bansal's journey as an author began with a deep-rooted passion for storytelling and a desire to amplify the voices of those who often go unnoticed. Growing up in Mumbai, a city teeming with diversity and stories waiting to be told, Rashmi developed a keen eye for the extraordinary in the ordinary. She recognized the power of stories to inspire, uplift, and ignite the spark of possibility within individuals.

With a degree in economics from Sophia College, Mumbai, and an

MBA from IIM Ahmedabad, Rashmi Bansal combined her academic knowledge with her passion for storytelling to carve her own path as an author and entrepreneur. Her journey would eventually lead her to become one of India's most celebrated writers in the genre of non-fiction motivational literature.

Rashmi Bansal's books have become a beacon of motivation, offering readers a glimpse into the lives of real people who have defied societal norms and overcome challenges to achieve greatness. Her unique narrative style and ability to weave compelling stories have made her books immensely popular among readers seeking inspiration and guidance.

In her debut book, "Stay Hungry Stay Foolish," Rashmi Bansal shares the inspiring stories of twenty-five entrepreneurs who dared to follow their passions and transform their dreams into reality. The book struck a chord with aspiring entrepreneurs, resonating with its message of perseverance, risk-taking, and the pursuit of purpose-driven work.

Continuing her quest to showcase extraordinary tales, Rashmi Bansal released subsequent books such as "I Have a Dream" and "Follow Every Rainbow," where she highlights the journeys of individuals who have overcome gender biases, societal expectations, and personal hardships to achieve their goals. These books have become empowering resources for women seeking to break free from the limitations imposed by society and pursue their dreams with unwavering determination.

Rashmi Bansal's commitment to empowering women shines through in her work. She has been a staunch advocate for gender equality and has used her platform to showcase the stories of women who have shattered glass ceilings and blazed new trails. Through her books, Rashmi has inspired women to embrace their ambitions, navigate challenges with resilience, and create their own paths to success.

Moreover, Rashmi Bansal's dedication to empowering women extends beyond her books. She has actively engaged in initiatives and platforms that promote gender equality and provide support to aspiring female entrepreneurs. Through her entrepreneurial ventures, including JAM (Just Another Magazine) and Bloody Good Book, Rashmi has created avenues for women to share their stories, connect with like-minded individuals, and foster a supportive ecosystem.

Rashmi Bansal's impact as an author and entrepreneur cannot be overstated. Her books have touched the lives of millions, providing a much-needed dose of motivation, encouragement, and guidance. Through her literary endeavors, she has helped individuals believe in their own potential and pursue their dreams fearlessly.

Rashmi's relentless efforts to empower women and amplify their voices have ignited a wave of change. Her work has fostered a society that values inclusivity, diversity, and the limitless potential of every individual, regardless of gender or background.

As Rashmi Bansal continues her journey as a writer and advocate for empowerment, her legacy will continue to inspire generations to come. Her words will echo in the hearts of readers, reminding them that with passion, perseverance, and unwavering belief in oneself, dreams can indeed be turned into reality.

"The world becomes a better place when women empower each other, celebrating their collective strength and achievements."

"An empowered woman is a catalyst for change; she shapes the future with her vision and determination."

♡♡♡

SEVENTEEN

Rukhmabai Raut: Unyielding Courage

Rukhmabai Raut was an Indian physician and feminist who lived from November 22, 1864, to September 25, 1955. She was born into a Marathi family to parents Janardhan Pandurang and Jayantibai. Rukhmabai's father passed away when she was two years old, and her mother remarried Dr. Sakharam Arjun, a renowned physician and social activist in Bombay.

At the age of 11, Rukhmabai was married to Dadaji Bhikaji, her step-father's cousin. The marriage agreement stipulated that Dadaji would live with Rukhmabai's family and be financially supported by them while he acquired an education and became a "good man." However, when Rukhmabai reached puberty and the traditional ritual consummation of the marriage was expected, her step-father, Dr. Sakharam Arjun, who had reformist tendencies, refused to permit early consummation.

This displeased Bhikaji, who was now 20 years old, and he resented the efforts of Rukhmabai's family to mold him into a "good man." He had no interest in education and preferred to live with his maternal uncle, Narayan Dhurmaji, despite the advice of Dr. Sakharam Arjun. Bhikaji's association with his uncle's household led him down a path of indolence and waywardness. Eventually, he accumulated debts and hoped to use Rukhmabai's property to repay them. However, Rukhmabai refused to move in with Bhikaji and chose to live with the support of her step-father.

During this time, Rukhmabai pursued her studies at home with books from a Free Church Mission library. She came into contact with influential figures such as Vishnu Shastri Pandit, a strong advocate for women's causes in Western India, and European men and women who exposed her to liberal reformism. She attended meetings of organizations like the Prarthanä Samäj and Arya Mahilä Samäj with her mother. Rukhmabai received support from various individuals, including Dr. Edith Pechey, who encouraged her and helped raise funds for her education. In 1889, Rukhmabai traveled to England to study medicine.

In 1894, Rukhmabai earned her Doctor of Medicine from the London School of Medicine for Women and the Royal Free Hospital. While Doctors Kadambini Ganguly and Anandi Gopal Joshi were the first Indian women to receive medical degrees in 1886, Rukhmabai became the second woman to both obtain a medical degree and practice medicine. She returned to India in 1895 and worked as the Chief Medical Officer at the Women's Hospital in Surat. Later, she declined an offer to work in the Women's Medical Service and instead chose to work at the Zenana (Women's) State Hospital in Rajkot until her retirement in 1929. Rukhmabai also established the Red Cross Society in Rajkot. After retiring, she settled in Bombay.

Rukhmabai is best known for her involvement in a landmark legal case related to her marriage as a child bride between 1884 and 1888. The case sparked significant public debate on topics such as law versus tradition, social reform versus conservatism, and feminism in both British-ruled India and England. The case ultimately contributed to the passing of the Age of Consent Act in 1891. In 1929, Rukhmabai published a pamphlet titled "Purdah - the need for its abolition," advocating for the active participation of young widows in Indian society.

Rukhmabai passed away at the age of 90 from lung cancer on September 25, 1955. Her legal case and contributions to women's rights were later documented in the book "Enslaved Daughters: Colonialism, Law, and Women's Rights" by Sudhir Chandra, published in 2008. In 2016, her story was adapted into a Marathi film titled "Doctor Rakhmabai." Rukhmabai's contributions have been recognized and celebrated, including a Google Doodle commemorating her 153rd birthday on November 22, 2017.

"Empowerment is the bridge that connects a woman's dreams to reality; it provides the stepping stones to success."

"A woman empowered is a community uplifted; her positivity and determination create a ripple effect of progress."

♡♡♡

EIGHTEEN

SHAHEEN MISTRI: ILLUMINATING MINDS

Shaheen Mistri, a beacon of hope and an agent of change, is a renowned social activist and the visionary founder of Teach For India. Born with a passion for education and a relentless drive to create positive change, Shaheen has dedicated her life to providing quality education to underprivileged children. This chapter delves into her inspiring journey, highlighting her transformative efforts and the lasting impact she has made on countless lives.

Shaheen Mistri's journey in the realm of education began with her own deep-rooted belief in the power of learning. Raised in Mumbai, India, she was fortunate to have access to quality education. However, Shaheen recognized that millions of children across the country were denied this fundamental right. This realization ignited a fire within her to create a more equitable education system.

In 2007, Shaheen Mistri founded Teach For India, an organization aimed at addressing educational inequity by recruiting and training passionate individuals to teach in underprivileged schools. Inspired by the Teach For America model, Shaheen set out on a mission to bridge the educational gap and transform the lives of marginalized children.

Under Shaheen Mistri's leadership, Teach For India has flourished into a movement that has impacted thousands of students and communities across the country. The organization recruits exceptional graduates and professionals, who are known as Fellows and places them in low-income schools for a two-year teaching commitment.

Through rigorous training, continuous support, and a commitment to educational excellence, Teach For India Fellows become catalysts of change in their classrooms. They strive to create inclusive, engaging, and student-centered learning environments, nurturing the academic and holistic development of their students.

Shaheen Mistri's vision for Teach For India goes beyond the classroom. She envisions a society where every child, regardless of their socio-economic background, has access to quality education and an opportunity to fulfill their potential. Teach For India also works on systemic change by engaging with various stakeholders, advocating for policy reforms, and fostering collaboration among schools, communities, and other organizations.

Shaheen Mistri's transformative efforts through Teach For India have garnered widespread recognition and praise. Her unwavering commitment to educational equity has earned her accolades such as the Skoll Award for Social Entrepreneurship and the Padma Shri, one of India's highest civilian honors. Her work has not only transformed the lives of individual students but has also influenced the broader discourse on education and social change.

Shaheen Mistri's impact extends beyond Teach For India. She has been actively involved in various social initiatives aimed at uplifting underprivileged communities. Through her foundation, Akanksha, she has worked to improve the quality of education in government schools and provide holistic support to children from low-income backgrounds.

Shaheen's advocacy for education equality has also led her to serve on several national and international boards and committees, shaping policies and strategies to ensure equitable access to education for all.

Shaheen Mistri's journey is a testament to the power of a single individual's vision and unwavering commitment to creating a more equitable society through education. Her transformative efforts through Teach For India have touched the lives of countless students, giving them hope, inspiration, and a pathway to a brighter future.

Shaheen Mistri's work continues to inspire and mobilize individuals, organizations, and policymakers to take collective action in addressing educational inequity. Her legacy serves as a reminder that education is not just a privilege but a fundamental right that must be accessible to all.

As Shaheen Mistri's journey unfolds, the impact of her tireless efforts and unwavering passion will continue to illuminate minds, break barriers, and create a ripple effect of change in the quest for education equality.

"Empowerment is the heartbeat of gender equality, pulsating with the rhythm of fairness and justice."

"A woman's worth cannot be measured; it is infinite, immeasurable, and invaluable. Empower her, and she'll enrich the world."

NINETEEN

SINDHUTAI SAPKAL: THE MOTHER OF ORPHANS

Sindhutai Sapkal, a name that resonates with love, compassion, and selflessness, is a remarkable social worker and activist who has dedicated her life to the welfare of abandoned and orphaned children. Fondly known as the "Mother of Orphans," Sindhutai Sapkal has emerged as a beacon of hope for countless children in need. This chapter delves into her inspiring journey, highlighting her unwavering determination, resilience, and the profound impact she has made on the lives of vulnerable children.

Sindhutai Sapkal's journey is marked by personal hardships and immense resilience. Born into a poor family in Pimpri Meghe, Maharashtra, India, she faced numerous challenges from a young age. Struggling with poverty, social stigma, and an abusive marriage, Sindhutai's life seemed enveloped in darkness. However, amidst the adversity, her inherent compassion and strength shone through.

Sindhutai's life took a transformative turn when she was

abandoned by her husband while pregnant. Determined to give her child a better life, she chose to embrace motherhood with unwavering love and courage. Sindhutai's unconditional love for her child planted the seeds of empathy within her, awakening a deep sense of responsibility towards other abandoned and orphaned children.

In the early 1970s, Sindhutai Sapkal founded the "Mann Vadis" (Mother's Home) organization, which later became the "Mother's Love Foundation." Through this initiative, Sindhutai opened her doors and her heart to abandoned and orphaned children, providing them with shelter, care, and most importantly, a mother's love. Her humble beginnings in a small hut soon grew into a haven for countless children in need.

Sindhutai Sapkal's relentless dedication and selflessness have left an indelible impact on the lives of abandoned children. She has opened her heart and home to more than 1,400 children over the years, ensuring they receive the love, care, and opportunities they deserve. Her unwavering commitment to their well-being has created a nurturing environment where children can flourish, reclaim their childhood, and pursue their dreams.

Beyond providing shelter and care, Sindhutai Sapkal's Foundation works tirelessly to ensure that every child receives an education and the necessary skills to lead independent lives. The organization focuses on empowering children with knowledge, values, and vocational training, enabling them to build a better future for themselves.

Sindhutai Sapkal's extraordinary efforts have garnered widespread recognition and acclaim. Her selfless service to society has earned her prestigious awards, including the Padma Shri, one of India's highest civilian honors. However, her truest reward lies in the countless lives she has touched, the smiles she has brought, and the hope she has instilled in the hearts of those she has nurtured.

Sindhutai Sapkal's legacy extends far beyond her own accomplishments. She has inspired countless individuals and organizations to come forward and contribute to the welfare of abandoned and orphaned children. Her story serves as a powerful reminder that a single individual's compassion and determination can make a profound difference in the lives of the most vulnerable.

Sindhutai Sapkal's journey as the "Mother of Orphans" is a testament to the transformative power of love, compassion, and unwavering dedication. Her selfless service has provided a lifeline to countless children, offering them a second chance at life and the belief that they are deserving of love and happiness.

As we reflect upon Sindhutai Sapkal's remarkable journey, let us be inspired to extend our own acts of kindness and embrace the spirit of compassion. Together, we can create a world where no child is left orphaned, and every child is embraced with a mother's love.

"Empowered women don't wait for opportunities; they create them, turning challenges into stepping stones."

"In the symphony of empowerment, every woman has a unique melody; together, they create a harmonious and empowering composition."

ღღღ

TWENTY

SUDHA CHANDRAN: DANCING AGAINST ALL ODDS:

Sudha Chandran, an epitome of resilience and determination, is an accomplished Indian classical dancer who defied all odds to pursue her passion for dance. Despite losing a leg in a tragic accident, she emerged as an inspiration for aspiring dancers and a symbol of indomitable spirit. This chapter explores Sudha Chandran's remarkable journey, highlighting her unwavering determination, her triumphant return to the stage, and the impact she has made on the world of dance.

Born on September 27, Sudha Chandran grew up in Mumbai, India, with an innate passion for dance. From a young age, she displayed exceptional talent and dedication, undergoing rigorous training in classical dance forms, particularly Bharatanatyam. Sudha's performances captivated audiences, and she seemed destined for a successful career as a dancer.

In 1981, tragedy struck Sudha Chandran's life when a bus accident resulted in the amputation of her right leg. The devastating loss could have shattered her dreams and dampened her spirit, but Sudha refused to let adversity define her. Instead, she turned it into a catalyst for personal growth and triumph.

Sudha Chandran's journey towards recovery was arduous, both physically and emotionally. With unwavering determination and the support of her family, she embarked on a path of rehabilitation and relearning. Through the use of a prosthetic limb, Sudha slowly regained her mobility, refusing to let her physical condition limit her aspirations.

Sudha Chandran's remarkable comeback to the world of dance showcased her tenacity and love for the art form. She adapted her choreography and dance techniques to accommodate her physical condition, harnessing the power of her upper body and facial expressions to compensate for her loss. Sudha's indomitable spirit and flawless performances left audiences in awe, breaking barriers and challenging societal perceptions of what is possible.

Sudha Chandran's story resonates with aspiring dancers worldwide, serving as a beacon of hope and inspiration. Her unwavering passion, coupled with her ability to overcome adversity, has motivated countless individuals to pursue their dreams relentlessly. Sudha's journey exemplifies the belief that true talent and dedication transcend physical limitations.

Sudha Chandran's accomplishments extend beyond her contributions to the world of dance. She is an accomplished actress, a renowned motivational speaker, and an advocate for the rights of persons with disabilities. Sudha has used her platform to raise awareness about inclusivity and to inspire others to embrace their uniqueness and overcome societal barriers.

Sudha Chandran's exceptional talent and remarkable journey have earned her numerous accolades and recognition. She has been honored with prestigious awards, including the National Award for Best Supporting Actress and the Woman Achiever Award. Her story has been documented in various media outlets, showcasing her resilience and inspiring millions around the world.

Sudha Chandran's legacy transcends the boundaries of dance and serves as a testament to the power of the human spirit. Her unwavering determination, coupled with her unmatched talent, has left an indelible impact on the world of dance and continues to inspire generations to follow their dreams fearlessly.

Sudha Chandran's journey is a testament to the indomitable spirit of the human soul. Despite facing unimaginable challenges, she transformed her tragedy into triumph, proving that the human spirit can soar above physical limitations. Sudha's story is a powerful reminder that with passion, perseverance, and an unwavering belief in oneself, one can overcome any obstacle and achieve greatness.

Through her artistry and unwavering dedication, Sudha Chandran has become a source of inspiration, empowering individuals to embrace their uniqueness and pursue their dreams relentlessly. Her legacy serves as a guiding light, reminding us that the power to create our own destinies lies within us all.

"Empowerment is the light that dispels the darkness of inequality, illuminating the path for generations to come."

"A woman empowered is a beacon of hope, a testament to the indomitable spirit that resides within every female soul."

♡♡♡

Citation And Reference

The views expressed in this book are solely those of the author and do not reflect the opinions of any organization or individual.

This book has been written after extensive research and analysis, which involved referencing various books, the internet as well as the author's study and practical experiences.

The author has taken great care to ensure that all information presented is accurate and properly cited to give credit to the sources. However, despite our best efforts, human errors may still occur. If any reader discovers any errors in this book, the author respectfully welcomes their feedback and encourages them to bring it to our attention.

Such feedback is valuable, and the author will take all necessary steps to correct any errors and improve the content of this book in future editions. Thank you for your understanding and support in this regard.

The author respects the right to freedom of speech and expression guaranteed by Article 19(1)(a) of the Constitution of India."

|| LOKAHA SAMASTHAHA SUKHINO BHAVANTU ||

www.ingramcontent.com/pod-product-compliance
Lightning Source LLC
LaVergne TN
LVHW091102150826
845673LV00002B/684

* 9 7 9 8 8 9 1 8 6 0 7 4 2 *